Crafts for
St. Patrick's Day

Crafts for St. Patrick's Day

by Kathy Ross
Illustrated by Sharon Lane Holm

Holiday Crafts for Kids
The Millbrook Press
Brookfield, Connecticut

Happy Birthday, Judie!
Love, Kathy and Sharon

Library of Congress Cataloging-in-Publication Data
Ross, Kathy (Katharine Reynolds) 1948–
Crafts for St. Patrick's Day / Kathy Ross: illustrated by Sharon Lane Holm.
p. cm. — (Holiday crafts for kids)
Summary: Presents twenty simple craft projects including a shamrock bird,
a leprechaun face mask, a shillelagh, and other items featuring various symbols of
the popular Irish holiday.
ISBN 0-7613-1306-0 (lib. bdg.)
1. Saint Patrick's Day decorations—Juvenile literature. 2. Handicraft—Juvenile
literature. [1. Saint Patrick's Day. 2. Handicraft.] I. Holm, Sharon Lane. ill.
II. Title. III. Series.
TT900.S25R67 1999
745.594'1—dc21 98-8022 CIP AC

Published by The Millbrook Press, Inc.
2 Old New Milford Road
Brookfield, Connecticut 06804

Contents

Happy
St. Patrick's Day!

St. Patrick's Day is always celebrated on March 17. It is believed that St. Patrick was a man who went to Ireland in the fifth century to spread the Christian faith. There is a legend about St. Patrick that says he drove the snakes out of Ireland. No one knows if this story is actually true or if the snakes are symbolic of the beliefs he wanted to replace with Christian beliefs. Today, St. Patrick is the patron saint of Ireland and St. Patrick's Day is an important religious holiday in that country.

For millions of people of Irish descent in the United States, St. Patrick's Day has become a more public celebration. Shamrock plants and paper shamrocks appear, and lots of people wear green to celebrate the spirit of the day. Leprechauns and rainbows with pots of gold at the end are all part of the fun. Many communities have parades to further add to the festivity of the day.

Have fun making these projects in celebration of St. Patrick's Day!

Tube Snake

St. Patrick is said to have driven the snakes out of Ireland.

Here is what you need:

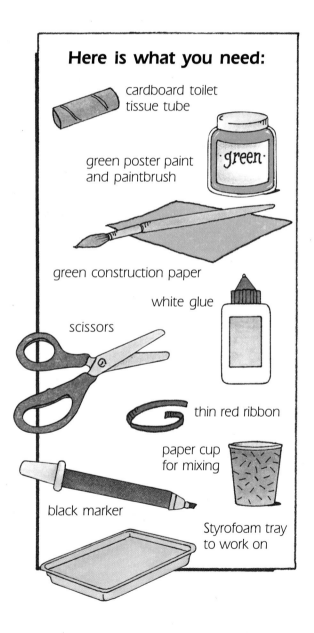

cardboard toilet tissue tube

green poster paint and paintbrush

green construction paper

white glue

scissors

thin red ribbon

paper cup for mixing

black marker

Styrofoam tray to work on

Here is what you do:

Mix four parts green paint with one part white glue in the paper cup. Paint both inside and outside of the tube with the paint-and-glue mixture. Let it dry on the Styrofoam tray. The glue in the paint will help the tube hold together when you cut it.

Start at one end of the cardboard tube and cut the tube in a spiral almost to the other end.

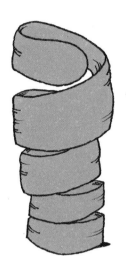

Leave a ring of cardboard at the end of the tube for a stand. Round off the end of the tube where you started to cut for the head of the snake.

 Cut a forked tongue for the snake from the red ribbon. Glue the tongue to the head end of the snake.

Draw two eyes on the head with the black marker.

Cut a 5-inch (13-centimeter) shamrock from the green paper. Glue the snake in the middle of the shamrock.

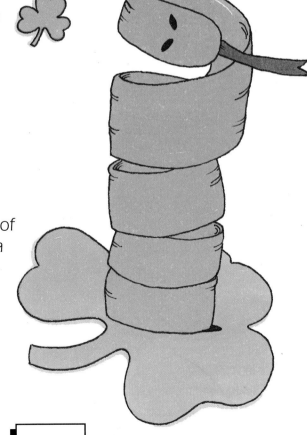

You might have to tell some of your friends why you made a snake for St. Patrick's Day.

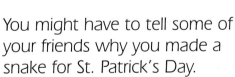

Candy Box Shamrock

Save those candy boxes from Valentine's Day in February
to make shamrocks for St. Patrick's Day in March.

Here is what you need:

two heart-shaped candy
boxes of similar size

plastic wrap
to work on

scissors

green poster
paint and a
paintbrush

white glue

paper cup
for mixing

gold glitter

green ribbon

hole punch

Here is what you do:

Take the lids off both
candy boxes so that you have
four heart shapes. Arrange three of
the hearts open side down on the
plastic wrap in the shape of a
shamrock.

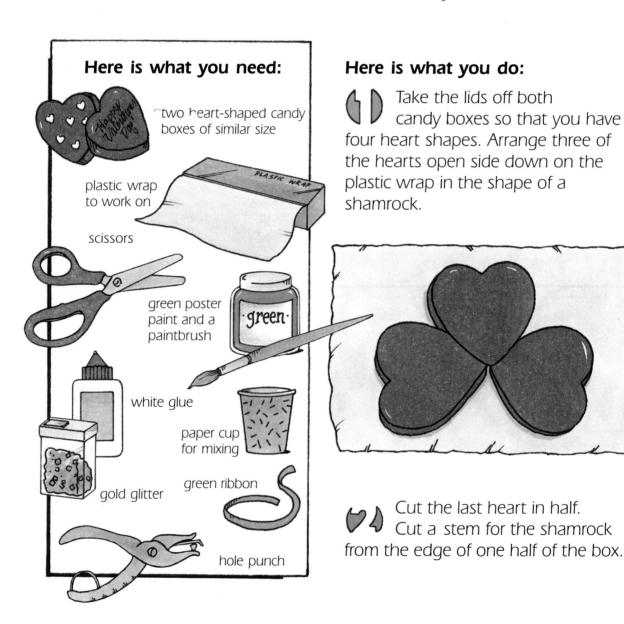

Cut the last heart in half.
Cut a stem for the shamrock
from the edge of one half of the box.

Put the stem at the bottom of the three shamrock leaves.

Mix four parts green paint with one part white glue in the paper cup. Paint the entire surface of the shamrock with the paint-and-glue mixture. Make sure the four parts of the shamrock overlap each other at the center so that they will dry attached.

Sprinkle the wet paint with gold glitter. Leave the project on the plastic wrap until it is completely dry. (If you try to do this project on newspaper instead of plastic wrap, you will end up with bits of newspaper stuck to the shamrock.)

Cut a 2-foot (60-centimeter) piece of green ribbon. Punch a hole on each side of the top shamrock petal. Thread the ribbon through the two holes and tie the ends together to make a hanger.

You can decorate this shamrock even more using lace, rick-rack, or other collage materials.

Stuffed Irish Friend

Make one or more of these Irish friends to celebrate
St. Patrick's Day with you!

Here is what you need:

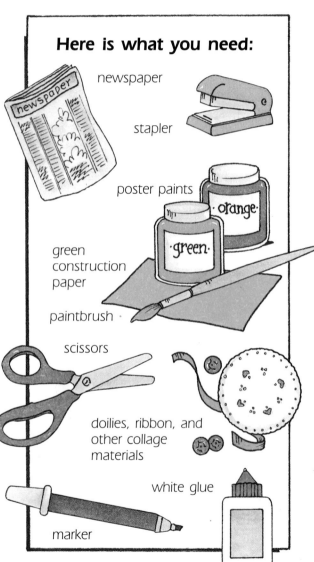

newspaper

stapler

poster paints

orange

green

green construction paper

paintbrush

scissors

doilies, ribbon, and other collage materials

white glue

marker

Here is what you do:

Stack two double sheets of newspaper on top of each other. Fold them to close them to four single sheets. Fold the stack of single sheets in half from top to bottom so that you now have a rectangle that is eight sheets thick.

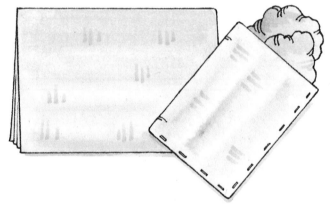

Staple across the bottom and up one side of the rectangle to make a bag with an opening. Stuff the bag with crumpled newspaper.

Staple the top of the bag shut. This will be the head and body of your Irish friend.

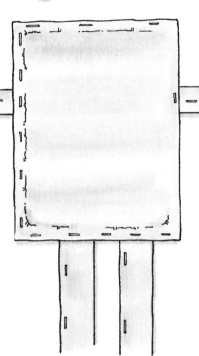

Roll single sheets of newspaper from side to side to make the legs. Staple the newspaper to hold the roll in place. Staple the two legs to the bottom of the body. If they seem too long, just trim them off with the scissors.

Roll single sheets of newspaper the short way to make the arms. Staple the roll to hold it in place. Staple an arm to each side of the body.

Use poster paints to draw a face and clothes. Use doilies and other collage materials to add details.

Cut a shamrock from the green paper. Use the marker to write a St. Patrick's Day message on it. Bring the two arms around in front of the body and staple the two ends together. Glue the shamrock to the hands.

Find a comfy chair for your new friend to sit in!

Irish Potato Puppet

The potato is an important food crop in Ireland.

Here is what you need:

brown, black, white, and green construction paper

scissors

white glue

green yarn

hole punch

cellophane tape

black and red markers

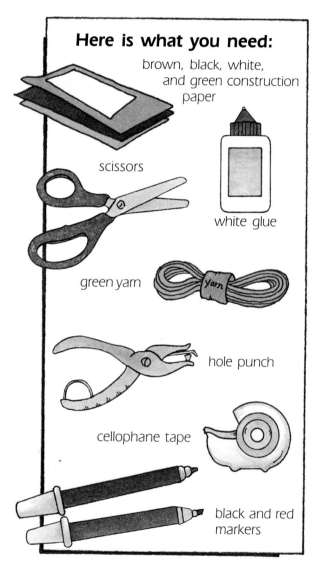

Here is what you do:

Fold the brown paper in half. Draw a potato that is large enough to fit over your hand.

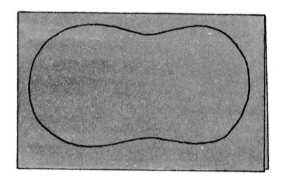

Cut around the shape on the folded paper so that you cut out a front and a back for the potato.

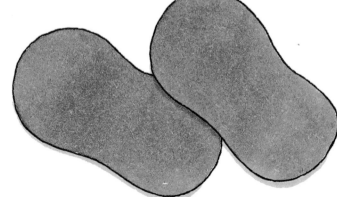

3 Holding the front and back of the potato together, punch holes around the sides and top. Make the holes about an inch apart.

4 Cut a 2-foot (60-centimeter) length of green yarn. Tie one end of the yarn to the first hole on one side of the potato. Wrap the other end of the yarn with the cellophane tape to make it stiff so that it is easier to thread through the holes.

5 Lace around the entire potato to sew it together. Tie off the yarn at the last hole and trim off any extra.

6 Cut eyes and a nose for the potato puppet from the black and white paper. Glue them in place on the top part of one side of the potato. Use the red marker to draw on a smile.

7 Cut a small shamrock from the green paper. Write a St. Patrick's Day message on it. Glue the shamrock to the potato.

You can decorate your potato puppet with more shamrocks or an Irish hat.

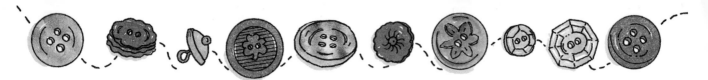

Button-Nose Shamrock

Your shirt button makes the nose for this little shamrock.

Here is what you need:

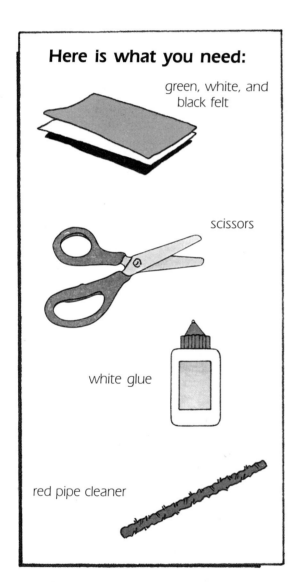

green, white, and black felt

scissors

white glue

red pipe cleaner

Here is what you do:

Cut a small shamrock from the green felt. Cut a ½-inch (1-centimeter) slit across the center of the shamrock for a button hole.

Cut eyes for the shamrock from the white and black felt. Glue the eyes to the top portion of the shamrock above the slit.

Cut a 1-inch (2½-centimeter) piece of red pipe cleaner. Bend the pipe cleaner into a smile. Glue the smile on the shamrock below the slit.

The nose for this happy shamrock will depend on what kind of buttons you are wearing when you wear it.

Shamrock Mouse Magnet

Surprise someone special with this little
mouse magnet for St. Patrick's Day.

Here is what you need:

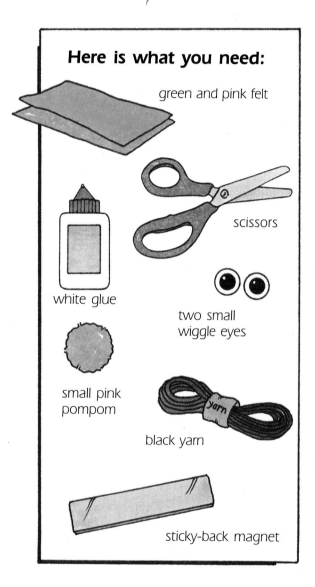

green and pink felt

scissors

white glue

two small
wiggle eyes

small pink
pompom

black yarn

sticky-back magnet

Here is what you do:

Cut a small shamrock from the
green felt. Turn the shamrock
so that the stem is at the top, forming
the mouse's tail. The two petals on
each side of the stem will be the ears
of the mouse.

Cut a pink liner for each ear
the pink felt. Glue the liners
to the ear petals of the shamrock.

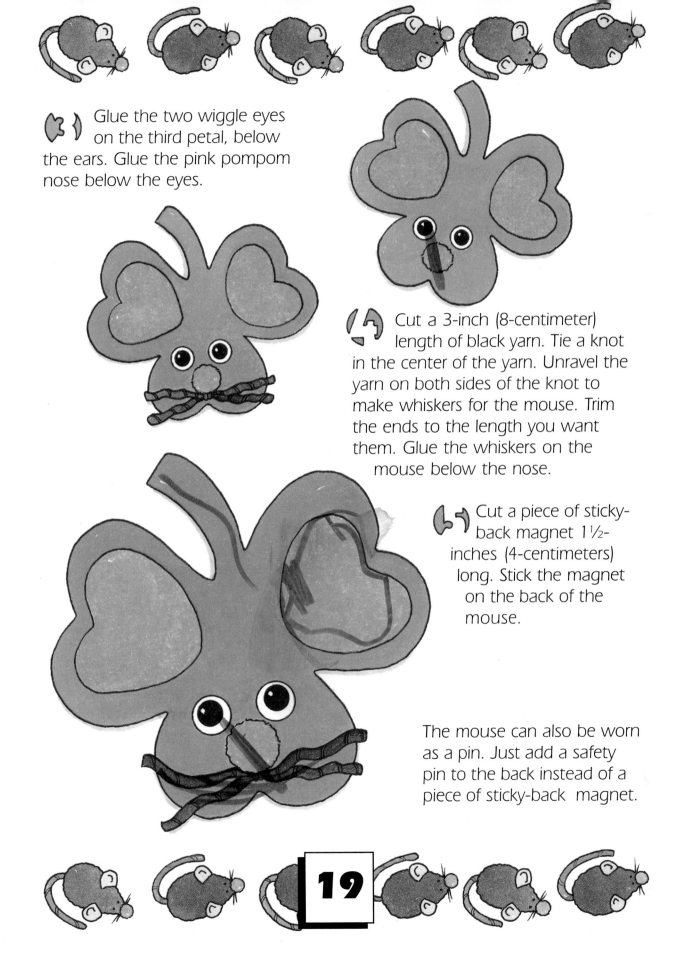

Glue the two wiggle eyes on the third petal, below the ears. Glue the pink pompom nose below the eyes.

Cut a 3-inch (8-centimeter) length of black yarn. Tie a knot in the center of the yarn. Unravel the yarn on both sides of the knot to make whiskers for the mouse. Trim the ends to the length you want them. Glue the whiskers on the mouse below the nose.

Cut a piece of sticky-back magnet 1½-inches (4-centimeters) long. Stick the magnet on the back of the mouse.

The mouse can also be worn as a pin. Just add a safety pin to the back instead of a piece of sticky-back magnet.

Shamrock Dog Pencil Holder

Make this shamrock dog to hold your pencils and pens.

Here is what you need:

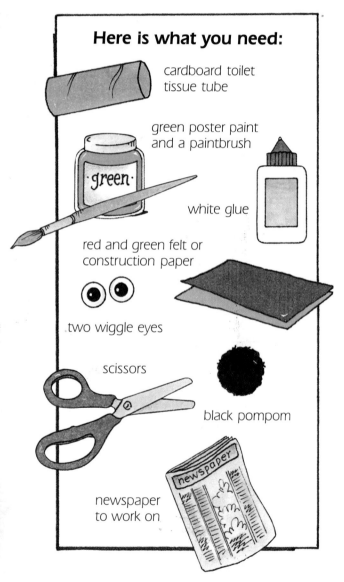

cardboard toilet tissue tube

green poster paint and a paintbrush

white glue

red and green felt or construction paper

two wiggle eyes

scissors

black pompom

newspaper to work on

Here is what you do:

Paint both the inside and the outside of the cardboard tube green. This will be the body of the dog and hold the pencils.

Cut a shamrock shape from green felt or paper.

Cut the stem off the shamrock. The shamrock part will be the head of the dog. Glue the stem to the bottom back of the tube for a tail.

Glue the two wiggle eyes to the face. Glue the black pompom below the eyes for a nose. Cut a tongue for the dog from red felt or paper. Glue it behind the edge of the shamrock and below the nose.

Cut a circle of green felt or paper to cover the opening at the bottom of the tube. Glue the circle to the tube to close the bottom.

ARF! That is dog talk for "Happy St. Patrick's Day!"

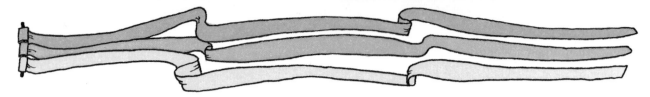

Shamrock Wand

Create a little St. Patrick's Day magic with this project!

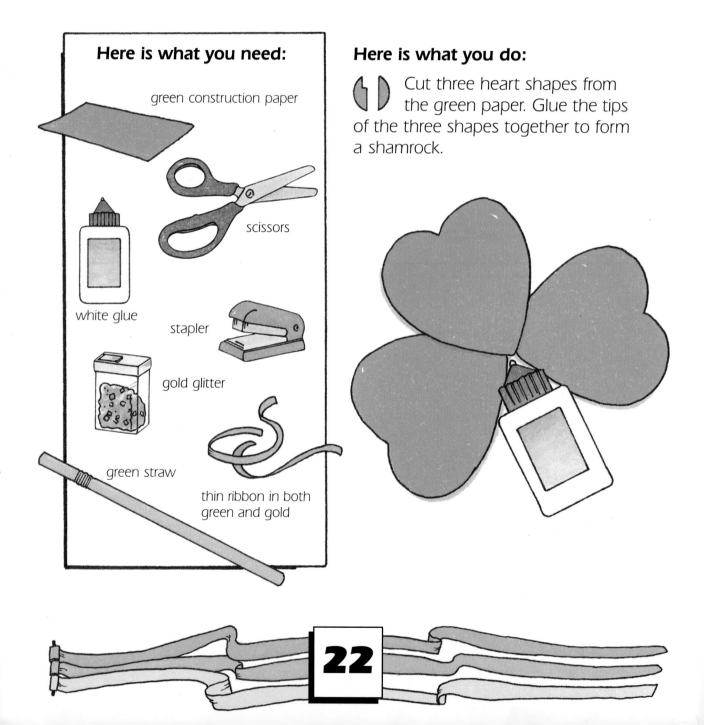

Here is what you need:

green construction paper

scissors

white glue

stapler

gold glitter

green straw

thin ribbon in both green and gold

Here is what you do:

Cut three heart shapes from the green paper. Glue the tips of the three shapes together to form a shamrock.

Staple the center of the shamrock to one end of the straw to make a handle.

Decorate the shamrock with gold glitter.

Cut three or more 3-foot (90-centimeter) ribbons. Hold the ribbons together and staple them to the back of the shamrock at the center so that the ends hang down from the shamrock wand.

Cut several tiny shamrocks and staple them along the ribbons.

Maybe your magic wand can help you catch a leprechaun!

Basket of Shamrocks Necklace

This basket of shamrocks looks like it belongs to one of the little people!

Here is what you need:

small plastic laundry product screw-cap, green if possible

yellow pipe cleaner

masking tape

white glue

scissors

gold glitter

green construction paper

green yarn

green ribbon

fiberfill or cotton balls

Here is what you do:

Put pieces of masking tape inside the cap to create a better gluing surface.

Cut a 10-inch (25-centimeter) piece of pipe cleaner. Wrap the two ends around each other to make a circle. Put the wrapped side of the circle into the cap and shape the pipe cleaner sticking out of the cap into a handle for the basket.

(3) Cover the bottom and sides of the inside of the cap with glue. Fill the cap about three quarters full of fiberfill or cotton balls.

(4) Cut some bits of green yarn and glue them over the cotton at the top of the basket to look like blades of grass.

(5) Cut some tiny shamrocks from the green construction paper. Glue the shamrocks tucked in among the yarn grass blades in the basket.

(6) Dab some glue on the grass and the shamrocks and sprinkle them with gold glitter.

(7) Cut a 3-foot (90-centimeter) piece of green ribbon. Thread one end of the ribbon through the handle of the basket, then tie the two ends together to make a necklace.

This project also makes a very nice table decoration. If you do not plan to wear it as a necklace, you can use a much larger cap for the basket.

Hand Leprechaun Card

Use a bit of Irish magic to turn your hand into a leprechaun.

Here is what you need:

piece of 9-inch by 12-inch (23- by 30-centimeter) yellow construction paper

marker

green, pink, and orange poster paint and a paintbrush

two wiggle eyes

white glue

pink pompom and orange pompom

newspaper to work on

Here is what you do:

Fold the yellow paper in half to make a 9-inch by 6-inch (23- by 15-centimeter) greeting card. Use the marker to write a St. Patrick's Day greeting inside the card. Don't forget to sign your name.

Happy St. Patrick's Day! from Dylan

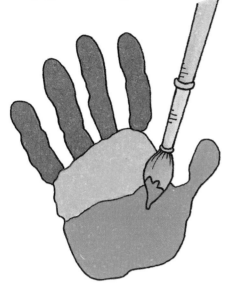

Paint the fingers of one of your hands orange for the beard of the leprechaun. Paint the strip of hand at the base of your fingers pink for the face. Paint the remainder of your hand and your thumb green to make the hat of the leprechaun.

You need to print your hand so that your fingers are at the bottom of the front of the card. To do this, you will need to turn the card upside-down. Carefully print on the card.

Glue two wiggle eyes and a pink pompom nose on the pink face of the leprechaun. Glue the orange pompom to the top of the thumb to make the hat look like a stocking cap.

You might want to write the date on this card so you can remember the year your hand was just the right size for making leprechauns.

March 1999

Stand-up
Shamrock Greeting

This greeting card stands up to wish everyone who
sees it a happy St. Patrick's Day!

Here is what you need:

green, white, black, and orange
construction paper

green tissue paper

scissors

stapler

hole punch

yellow pompom

markers

cereal box
cardboard

white glue

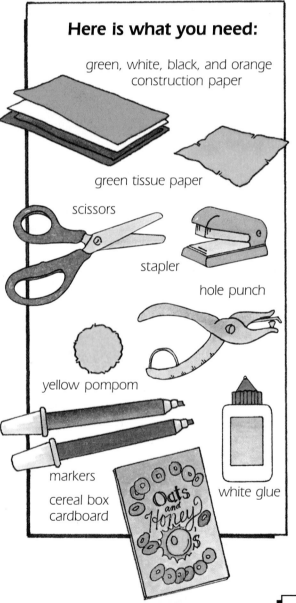

Here is what you do:

Cut a shamrock from the green
paper that is about 9 inches (23
centimeters) across. Cut an identical
shamrock from the green tissue paper.

Punch holes around the
construction paper shamrock
and down the stem.

(3) Glue the green tissue shamrock behind the construction paper shamrock so that the tissue shows through the holes.

(4) Cut eyes for the shamrock from the black and white paper. Glue the eyes to the front, top part of the shamrock. Glue the yellow pompom below the eyes for a nose. Use a red marker to give the shamrock a great big smile.

(5) Cut a square of orange paper that is about as wide and as tall as the shamrock. Write a St. Patrick's Day message across the bottom edge of the square and sign your name.

(6) Cut a strip of cereal box cardboard 2 inches (5 centimeters) wide and as tall as the shamrock. Staple one end of the strip to the top of the back of the shamrock. Lay the shamrock face down over the square and, being careful to keep the stem free, staple the other end of the strip to the back of the square.

To stand the shamrock up, just pull the bottom of the shamrock forward and stand it on its stem and side leaves. The cardboard strip will support it.

Shamrock Bird

Have you ever heard of a shamrock bird?

Here is what you need:

green, orange, white, and black construction paper

scissors

white glue

marker

Here is what you do:

Cut two identical shamrocks from the green paper.

Fold the orange paper and cut a beak for the bird on the fold so that the top and bottom of the folded paper form the top and bottom of the beak. Cut two legs for the bird from orange paper.

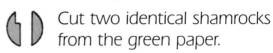

legs

beak

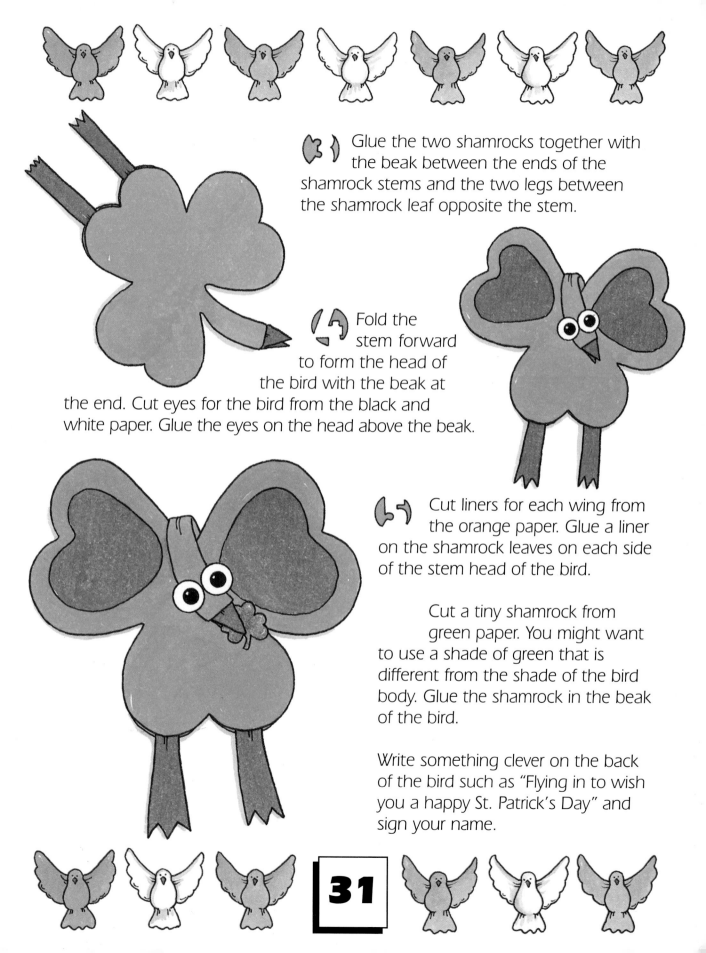

Glue the two shamrocks together with the beak between the ends of the shamrock stems and the two legs between the shamrock leaf opposite the stem.

Fold the stem forward to form the head of the bird with the beak at the end. Cut eyes for the bird from the black and white paper. Glue the eyes on the head above the beak.

Cut liners for each wing from the orange paper. Glue a liner on the shamrock leaves on each side of the stem head of the bird.

Cut a tiny shamrock from green paper. You might want to use a shade of green that is different from the shade of the bird body. Glue the shamrock in the beak of the bird.

Write something clever on the back of the bird such as "Flying in to wish you a happy St. Patrick's Day" and sign your name.

Leprechaun Face Mask

Disguise yourself as a leprechaun on St. Patrick's Day!

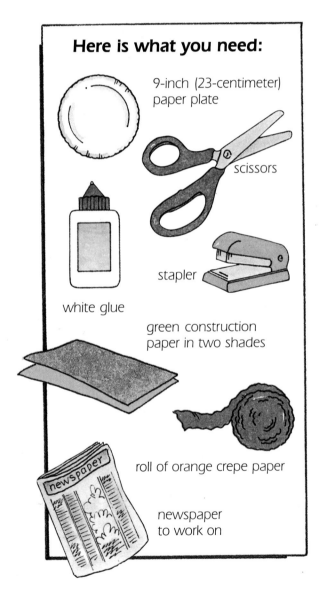

Here is what you need:

9-inch (23-centimeter) paper plate

scissors

white glue

stapler

green construction paper in two shades

roll of orange crepe paper

newspaper to work on

Here is what you do:

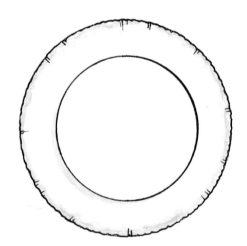

Cut the center out of the paper plate. This will be the front of the face mask.

Cut about twelve 14-inch (36-centimeter) strips of crepe paper. Glue them around the bottom of the plate rim for a beard. Cut some longer strips to glue on each side of the plate for hair.

Cut a hat for the mask from one of the shades of green paper. Cut several small shamrocks from the other shade of green paper. Use them to decorate the hat. Glue the hat to the top of the face mask.

Cut a band of green paper about 2 inches (5 centimeters) wide and 18 inches (46 centimeters) long. Staple one end of the band to the top of the face mask behind the hat. Bring the band around the back of your head so that the mask fits comfortably and staple the strip to the other side of the mask. Trim off any extra strip.

Put on your mask and start practicing the Irish jig!

Shillelagh

The shillelagh is a stick used for walking that is carved from wood found in the Shillelagh Forest in Ireland.

Here is what you need:

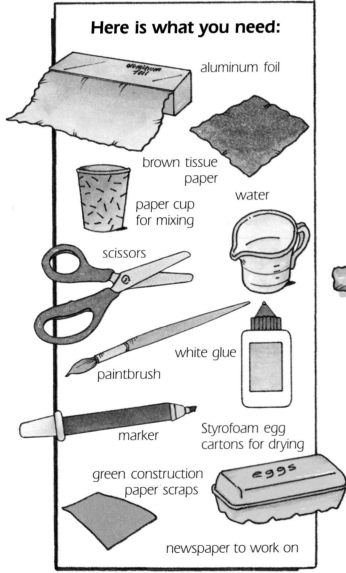

aluminum foil

brown tissue paper

paper cup for mixing

water

scissors

paintbrush

white glue

marker

Styrofoam egg cartons for drying

green construction paper scraps

newspaper to work on

Here is what you do:

Tear off a 30-inch (76-centimeter) strip of aluminum foil. Squeeze the foil together along the strip to form a stick. Tear off a second strip of foil of about the same length. Wrap and squeeze the second strip around the foil stick to make it thicker.

Cut squares of brown tissue to wrap around the stick to cover it. You will want to do at least two layers of wrapped tissue to give the stick a dark brown color.

Mix four parts glue with one part water in the paper cup. Paint the stick with the watery glue and wrap it with the tissue, pressing the tissue into the glue and

foil to give it a rough carved look. Paint the outside of the tissue with more watery glue. Repeat this step to give the shillelagh a second layer of tissue paper. Bend one end to make a handle.

Do not leave the shillelagh on the newspaper to dry. Prop it up over the newspaper on Styrofoam egg cartons or it will stick to the newspaper and spoil the surface of the project.

To identify your own shillelagh you can add your initials to it. Cut out two tiny shamrocks and put your first initial on one and your second initial on the other. Glue them on the shillelagh just below the handle.

This shillelagh is just the thing to carry when you are wearing the leprechaun mask found on page 32.

Pot of Gold
Table Decoration

Some say there is a pot of gold at the end of the rainbow.

Here is what you need:

2½-inch (6-centimeter) Styrofoam ball

black poster paint and a paintbrush

·black·

white glue

scissors

black pipe cleaner

red, gold, green, and blue sparkle stems

fiberfill

old gold pierced earrings

Styrofoam tray to work on

Here is what you do:

Ask an adult to cut the top ¼ inch (½ centimeter) off the Styrofoam ball and just enough off the bottom so that it is flat enough to stand upright. This will be the pot.

Paint the pot black and let it dry.

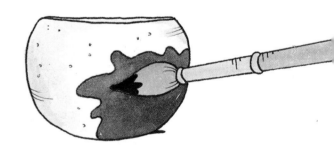

Wrap the piece of the black pipe cleaner around the opening of the pot and stick the two ends into the Styrofoam to hold it in place. Cut two black handles for the

pot from the rest of the pipe cleaner and stick them in the Styrofoam on each side of the pot.

Cut the sparkle stems about 6 inches (15 centimeters) long. Stick them in the Styrofoam at the back of the pot with the red first, then gold, green, and blue. If you try to use more rainbow colors, the pot will tip backwards instead of standing up.

Curve the sparkle stems away from the pot to look like the arch of a rainbow. Glue a fluff of fiberfill around the top ends to look like a cloud.

Press the posts of the earrings into the Styrofoam on top of the pot to fill it with gold.

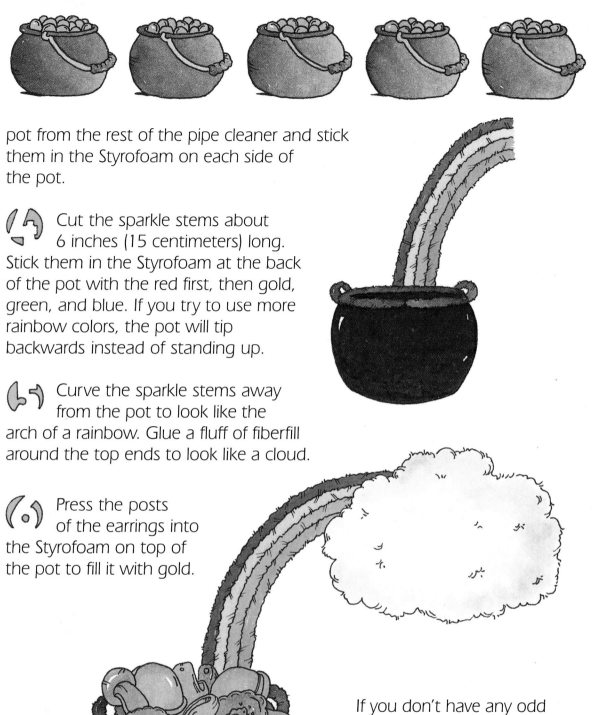

If you don't have any odd earrings, try gold buttons with shanks that could press into the Styrofoam. You can also fill the pot by gluing on wrapped gold candies or glitter.

Rainbow Bracelet

Make a rainbow to wear on your wrist.

Here is what you need:

cardboard tube

white glue

scissors

green poster paint

green

paintbrush

masking tape

hole punch

black sharp marker

tops from fat markers in red, orange, yellow, green, blue, and purple

scrap of white construction paper

seven tiny red pompoms or beads

thin green ribbon

Styrofoam tray for drying

newspaper to work on

Here is what you do:

Cut a 1¾-inch (4½-centimeter) ring off one end of the tube. Cut a slit down the cardboard ring to open it to make a cuff bracelet. Punch a hole in each side of the slit.

Paint the bracelet green on the inside and the outside and let it dry.

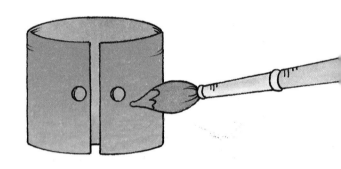

Line up the seven marker tops in this order: purple, blue, green, yellow, orange, and red. Put a strip of masking tape across the tops

to hold them together in a row. Turn the tops over so that the order from left to right is red, orange, yellow, green, blue, purple, and the masking tape is on the back.

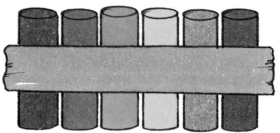

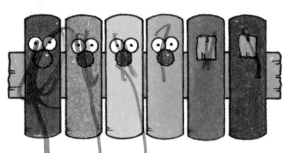

Punch out two eyes for each top from the white paper. Use the black marker to draw a pupil in the center of each eye. Glue two eyes on each color top. Glue a red pompom or bead nose just below each pair of eyes.

Put a tiny piece of masking tape on the top front of each marker top to make a better gluing surface for the face.

Glue the row of marker tops around the cuff bracelet.

Cut a 10-inch (25-centimeter) length of green ribbon. Thread an end through both holes punched in the bracelet and tie the ends together. The ribbon allows the bracelet to be adjusted to the size of the wrist of the person wearing it.

At last, something to do with all those tops from dried up markers!

Lucky Penny Necklace

With this project you can wear your lucky penny for St. Patrick's Day.

Here is what you need:

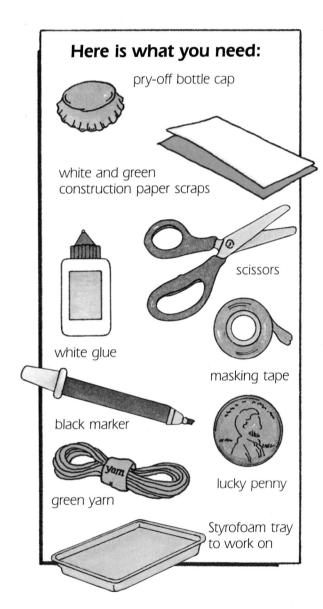

pry-off bottle cap

white and green construction paper scraps

scissors

white glue

masking tape

black marker

green yarn

lucky penny

Styrofoam tray to work on

Here is what you do:

Cut a circle from the white paper just large enough to cover the outside of the cap. Put a piece of masking tape on the cap to create a better gluing surface. Glue the white circle on the cap.

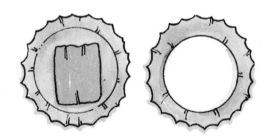

Cut a shamrock from the green paper small enough to fit on the white circle. If you wish, you can give the shamrock a happy face with the black marker.

40

Glue the shamrock to the paper-covered top of the cap.

Turn the cap over. Put a piece of masking tape over the inside of the cap. Put another piece of tape on the lucky penny. The tape will give the cap and the penny a better gluing surface. Glue the penny inside the cap. Let the project dry on the Styrofoam tray.

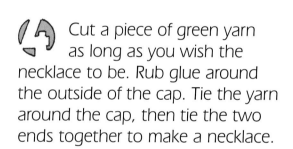

Cut a piece of green yarn as long as you wish the necklace to be. Rub glue around the outside of the cap. Tie the yarn around the cap, then tie the two ends together to make a necklace.

Wear your new necklace shamrock side out with your lucky penny hidden behind it.

Irish Castle Party Favor

Fill this castle with treats to make a St. Patrick's Day party favor.

Here is what you need:

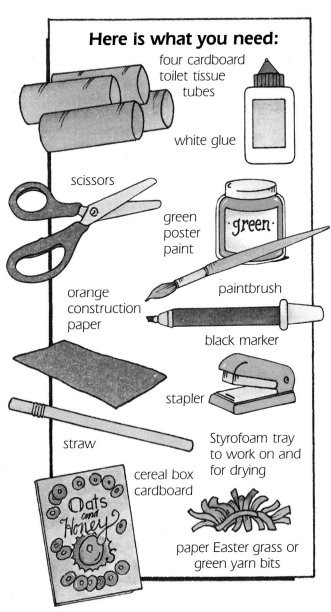

four cardboard toilet tissue tubes

white glue

scissors

green poster paint

paintbrush

orange construction paper

black marker

stapler

straw

Styrofoam tray to work on and for drying

cereal box cardboard

paper Easter grass or green yarn bits

Here is what you do:

Cut eight evenly spaced slits around one end of two of the cardboard tubes. Make the slits 1-inch (2½-centimeters) long. Fold in every other tab on the tubes to form turrets for the castle.

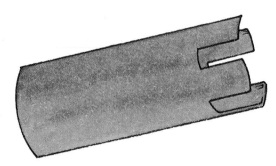

Glue the two uncut tubes together with one in front and the other in back. Glue the turrets on each side of the other two tubes. Let the glue dry on the Styrofoam tray.

Paint the castle green.

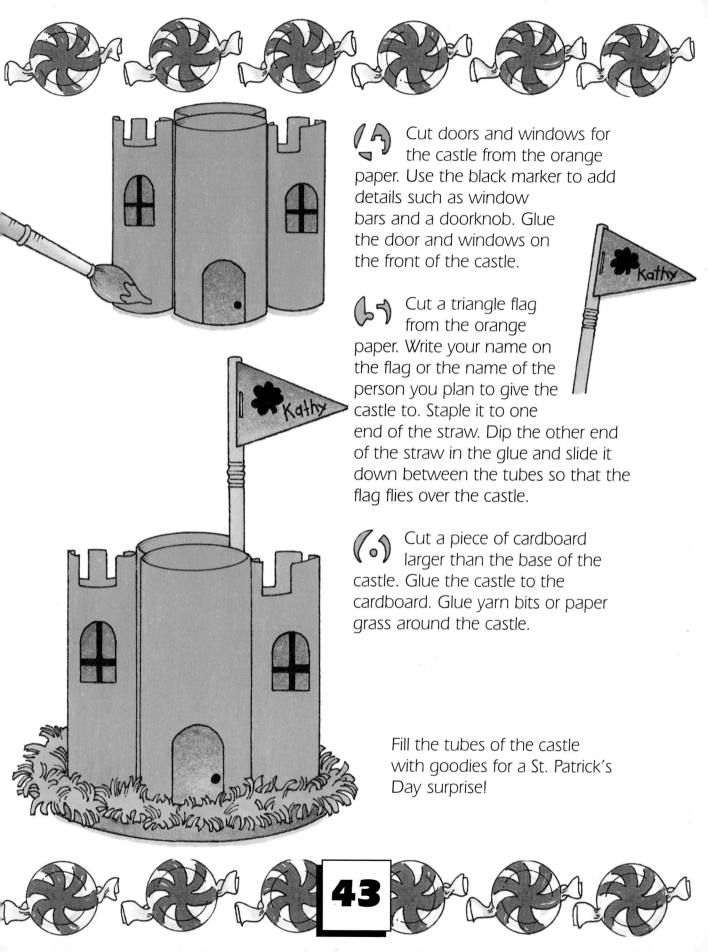

Cut doors and windows for the castle from the orange paper. Use the black marker to add details such as window bars and a doorknob. Glue the door and windows on the front of the castle.

Cut a triangle flag from the orange paper. Write your name on the flag or the name of the person you plan to give the castle to. Staple it to one end of the straw. Dip the other end of the straw in the glue and slide it down between the tubes so that the flag flies over the castle.

Cut a piece of cardboard larger than the base of the castle. Glue the castle to the cardboard. Glue yarn bits or paper grass around the castle.

Fill the tubes of the castle with goodies for a St. Patrick's Day surprise!

Shamrock Angel

Make this shamrock angel for someone special.

Here is what you need:

light green, dark green, and white construction paper

scissors

construction paper in skin tone of your choice

white glue

markers

yarn in hair color of your choice

masking tape

gold glitter

thin green ribbon

gold sparkle stem

Here is what you do:

Cut two identical shamrocks about 8 inches (20 centimeters) across. Cut one from the white paper and one from the green paper.

Cut a 3-inch (8-centimeter) circle from the skin-colored paper for the head.

Cut the two side leaves from the green shamrock, leaving the stem. Glue the green leaf over the center leaf of the white shamrock so that the green leaf forms the dress of an angel

and the two white leaves the wings. Glue the head on over the stems.

 Use the markers to draw a face on the angel. Glue yarn bits on the head for hair.

Shape a halo for the angel from the sparkle stem. Glue the stem of the halo to the back of the head. Use masking tape to hold the halo in place while the glue dries.

Cut tiny shamrocks and glue them on the angel's dress. Tie a bow with the green ribbon to glue at the neck of the angel. Decorate the wings and the dress with gold glitter.

Write "Happy St. Patrick's Day from your little angel" on the back and sign your name.

Door Leprechaun

This cheerful leprechaun will look terrific on your front door.

Here is what you need:

green, light green, black, yellow, red, and pink construction paper

scissors

red and black markers

green yarn

white glue

orange powdered tempera*

cotton balls

hole punch

lunch bag

* If you do not have any powdered tempera, you can give your leprechaun a white beard or dab it with orange water color paint.

Here is what you do:

Cut a sheet of 9-inch by 12-inch (23- by 30-centimeter) green paper in half lengthwise. Glue the two pieces together at the top end so that they hang down to form the legs of the leprechaun.

Cut a second sheet of 9-inch by 12-inch green paper in half lengthwise. Fold one of the pieces in half lengthwise and glue the fold to

form arms. Cut two hands from the pink paper. Slip a hand between the glued paper at each end. Glue the arms across the top of the legs.

Cut two boots and a belt from the black paper. Glue the top of each boot behind the end of each leg. Glue the belt across the middle of the leprechaun. Cut a buckle for the belt from the yellow paper and glue it in place. Cut shamrocks from the light green paper to trim the boots and belt.

Cut a 6-inch (15-centimeter) circle from the pink paper for a head. Cut two round eyes from the black paper. Use the hole punch to punch out a pupil in each eye. Glue the eyes to the head.

Cut a round red nose from the red paper. Glue it on the face below the eyes. Use the red marker to give the leprechaun a big smile.

To make a beard, shake about 16 cotton balls in the brown bag with a tablespoon of orange powdered tempera to color them orange. Glue the beard around the face.

Cut a hat from the green paper. Trim the hat with a black paper band and one or more shamrocks. Glue the hat on the leprechaun's head. Glue the head to the body of the leprechaun.

Cut a 2-foot (60-centimeter) length of green yarn. Glue an end of the yarn in each of the leprechaun's hands so that the yarn hangs across the front of him. Cut nine shamrocks from the light green paper. Glue the shamrocks, evenly spaced, across the yarn. Write "Good Luck" on the shamrocks, leaving one shamrock blank between the two words.

About the author and illustrator

Twenty-five years as a teacher and director of nursery school programs has given Kathy Ross extensive experience in guiding young children through crafts projects. Among the more than twenty-five craft books she has written are **Gifts to Make For Your Favorite Grownup, Crafts From Your Favorite Fairy Tales, The Best Holiday Crafts Ever!**, and **Crafts for Kids Who Are Wild About the Wild**.

Sharon Lane Holm, a resident of New Fairfield, Connecticut, won awards for her work in advertising design before shifting her concentration to children's books. Among the books she has illustrated recently are **Sidewalk Games** and **Happy Birthday, Everywhere!**, both by Arlene Erlbach, and **Beautiful Bats** by Linda Glaser.

Together, Kathy Ross and Sharon Lane Holm have also created **The Best Birthday Parties Ever: A Kid's Do-It-Yourself Guide, Christmas Ornaments Kids Can Make**, the popular "Holiday Crafts for Kids" series, as well as the "Crafts for Kids Who Are Wild About" series.